"*Equipping Grandparents* contains practical and biblical advice for pastors and grandparents who want to impact the next generation with the Gospel. A wonderful resource!"

—Chuck Swindoll

"We're so grateful that grandparents have the Legacy Coalition to coach them on how to use their influence to embed the gift of God's grace into a new generation."

—Tim Kimmel, founder and executive director, Family Matters; author, *Grace-Based Parenting*

"*Equipping Grandparents* is an essential primer to grandparenting ministry. Its writers are vetted leaders and pioneers in the 'grandparenting movement.' If you are looking for a resource to jump-start your efforts in establishing an outreach program in your church, buy this book."

—Ken Canfield, founder, National Center for Fathering and National Association of Grandparents; author, *7 Secrets of Effective Fathers*

EQUIPPING
GRANDPARENTS

Titles in the GRANDPARENTING MATTERS Series

EQUIPPING GRANDPARENTS

Helping Your Church Reach and Disciple the Next Generation

DR. JOSH MULVIHILL
GENERAL EDITOR

WITH CONTRIBUTIONS BY

Larry Fowler, Wayne Rice, John Coulombe, Joanne Lundberg,
Sherry Schumann, Cavin Harper, and Lynda Freeman

BETHANYHOUSE

a division of Baker Publishing Group
Minneapolis, Minnesota

Published by Bethany House Publishers
11400 Hampshire Avenue South
Bloomington, Minnesota 55438
www.bethanyhouse.com

Bethany House Publishers is a division of
Baker Publishing Group, Grand Rapids, Michigan

Printed in the United States of America

ISBN 978-0-7642-3130-8

Library of Congress Control Number: 2018940589

Unless otherwise indicated, Scripture quotations are from The Holy Bible, English Standard Version® (ESV®), copyright © 2001 by Crossway, a publishing ministry of Good News Publishers. Used by permission. All rights reserved. ESV Text Edition: 2011

Scripture quotations identified AMPC are from the Amplified® Bible, copyright © 1954, 1958, 1962, 1964, 1965, 1987 by The Lockman Foundation. Used by permission. (www.Lockman.org)

Scripture quotations identified NET are from the NET Bible®, copyright © 1996–2006 by Biblical Studies Press, L.L.C. http://netbible.com. Used by permission. All rights reserved.

Scripture quotations identified NIV quotations are from the Holy Bible, New International Version®. NIV®. Copyright © 1973, 1978, 1984, 2011 by Biblica, Inc.™ Used by permission of Zondervan. All rights reserved worldwide. www.zondervan.com

Scripture quotations identified NIV 1984 taken from the HOLY BIBLE, NEW INTERNATIONAL VERSION®. Copyright © 1973, 1978, 1984 Biblica. Used by permission of Zondervan. All rights reserved.

Cover design by Dan Pitts

Author is represented by William Denzel.

18   19   20   21   22   23   24   7   6   5   4   3   2   1

CONTENTS

PREFACE

Equipping Grandparents was written by family ministry experts to encourage church leaders to think about a demographic that has been overlooked and under-resourced in most churches: grandparents.

Take a moment and consider two questions. First, when was the last time your church addressed grandparenting from the pulpit or in a classroom? Second, what resources do you provide grandparents in your church to help them reach and disciple future generations? If your church is like most, individuals are left to figure out how to grandparent without the support of church leaders. The silence of most churches combined with the powerful messages grandparents hear from culture may have contributed to role confusion and minimized a grandparent's influence. Imagine the impact if millions of Christian grandparents were given a biblical vision for their place and purpose in the family.

Research reveals grandparents have a large influence on the faith of children, second only to parents. In addition, grandparents have been given a God-ordained role in the Bible. Deuteronomy 4:9 instructs us to teach these things "to your children and your children's children." This book will help church leaders equip grandparents to use their influence to pass faith on to future generations.

It is important for you to know what kind of book this is. Some books provide biblical insight. Others provide practical guidance. While there will be some biblical instruction, the majority of this book fits in the latter category. It is more of a "how-to" book than a "what" book. Once ministry leaders catch a vision for the biblical role of grandparents, the next question often asked is, "What resources are available to help me encourage grandparents to intentionally invest in the spiritual life of grandchildren?" That is why we created this resource.

Larry Fowler has written two chapters that address why a grandparent ministry is important and how to start one at your church. Larry served with Awana for three decades and uses this valuable experience to help you customize something that will work for your church. I (**Josh Mulvihill**) will introduce you to the biblical role of grandparenting and the competing messages of culture. I have served as a pastor in family ministry roles for nearly twenty years and did my PhD research on the biblical role of grandparents.

Wayne Rice provides a practical chapter about creating an intergenerational climate at your church. Wayne's advice is not theoretical. Wayne served in the trenches as a pastor and helped his church create the DNA he talks about in chapter 4.

John Coulombe and **Joanne Lundberg** have written chapters describing how they began grandparent ministries in their churches and provide ideas that may be transferable to your church. John is a pastor and Joanne has served in church-based children and family ministry for decades. They have pioneered grandparenting ministry models for the local church to build upon.

If you are a grandparent and want to know how to cast a vision to your pastor, then the article by **Sherry Schumann** may be helpful for you. Sherry serves as the prayer coordinator for the Christian Grandparenting Network. **Cavin Harper** has been training grandparents for almost two decades and encourages pastors to expand their vision for ministry to include grandparents.

Lynda Freeman has compiled a list of books that help grandparents effectively invest in their grandchildren. I have compiled a list of resources grandparents can use to disciple grandchildren. These lists are not meant to be exhaustive, but they provide a good starting point.

Together, these ten chapters offer a quick how-to manual and helpful resources to assist you and your church in reaching and discipling the youngest generation.

—Josh Mulvihill

1

Why Grandparenting Matters

LARRY FOWLER

I eagerly shared my newfound vision to start a grandparent ministry with a pastor and he responded by stating, "I'm not sure we need a grandparenting ministry. We already have an active senior adults group." It wasn't the first time I'd heard this response, and I knew this pastor needed help understanding who grandparents are (grandparents are not synonymous with senior saints), what Scripture has to say about the role of grandparents, and the incredible opportunity to launch an army of potential disciplers upon our youngest generations.

Maybe you're wondering the same thing as that pastor, *Why should my church start a grandparenting ministry?* Is grandparenting really that complicated? Does it really need an emphasis? This chapter will answer these questions.

The Objectives of a Grandparenting Ministry

We have two phrases that describe our desired outcome. The first is for you to become an *Intentional Christian Grandparent*.

That phrase describes the transformation that we would like to see in you as an individual. Likely, if you are reading this book, you are already a grandparent. In fact, you are probably a *Christian* grandparent. Maybe it has never occurred to you to be *intentional* in passing on your faith heritage. Our desire is that all grandparents would take the step into intentionality. It may be a simple step for some and difficult for others. Taking that step may be complicated by mixed-up relationships, hindered by barriers of all kinds, but its potential for good is too great to ignore.

A second phrase is *Grandparenting Matters*.

Yes, it *does* matter! Grandparenting Matters is our message to the local church and its leaders. The grandparent-grandchild relationship is worthy of attention and resources.

Few churches would overlook the parent-child relationship, and rightfully so. In the last couple of decades, much has been made of the scriptural mandate that *parents* are responsible for the spiritual upbringing of children, not the church. Parachurch ministries have sprung up because of this truth. There have been countless resources created to assist parents and to equip the church to train parents. I believe church leaders understand that parenting matters! But so does grandparenting, and we want church leaders to see that as well.

Six Reasons to Start a Grandparenting Ministry

Here are six reasons for a local church to start a grandparenting ministry and a grandparent to become intentional about passing on faith to their grandchildren.

1. Because of what Scripture says

Grandparents are to pass on a spiritual heritage to their grandchildren because it is biblical.

You'll learn about the biblical role of grandparents in chapter 2 from my friend and colleague Dr. Josh Mulvihill, but let me get us started. Scripture has numerous themes concerning the role of grandparents. I summarize three of them with the 1/2/4 principle to describe our interactions across generations.

Here are three general responsibilities of grandparents:

Watch one

Grandparents are given specific instructions about what to do in Deuteronomy 4:9 (NIV): "Only be careful,

15

and watch yourselves closely so that you do not forget the things your eyes have seen or let them fade from your heart as long as you live. Teach them to your children and to their children after them."

"Watch *yourselves*." We are to keep an eye on our generation! When we're tempted to focus on the problems, attitudes, or immaturity of the younger generations, this verse reminds us to look in the mirror. We are not to suffer decline in our spiritual health or our spiritual fervor. The grandparent stage of life ought to be when we are *most* kind, *most* faith-filled, *most* loving, *most* Christ-like. It's the time of life when we ought to be the quickest to forgive. Grandparents ought to be the least cranky, least cynical, least argumentative, and least impatient.

Is it any wonder that this command is first? After all, how we live our faith is a critically important factor in passing on our faith, isn't it?

Teach two

Deuteronomy 4:9 communicates a second theme regarding grandparenting responsibilities: We are to teach both our children and our grandchildren. God used this verse to rock my world and help me to see grandparenting differently.

"Teach them to your children *and* to their children after them."

Notice that it doesn't say we are to teach our children and then they teach their children after them. Grandparenting is not a relay-race process where we run our faith-training leg, pass the baton, and then go sit down. We're not done when we pass the responsibility on. The *and* tells us so much. It means we have a two-generation responsibility for intentionally teaching faith. We can't say, "We tried to do our job, kids. Now we're done and it's up to you."

Make no mistake, it *is* up to them. Our adult children have the primary responsibility to spiritually train their children. The faith-training baton *has* been passed to them. That is made abundantly clear in many places in Scripture. But our responsibility doesn't stop; it merely changes. We are to teach our children *and* our grandchildren. The little word *and* is a very important word. With it in there, we can't go sit down and watch after we've run our generational leg of the race. We are to teach *two* generations.

Diane and I were living in the Chicago area when we began to study Deuteronomy 4:9 and realize these truths. God began to stir our hearts. We have two sets of grandkids; our daughter, Andrea, and her family live in Colorado, and our son, Ryan, was starting his family in Southern California.

I kept thinking, *I can't do this. I can't live hundreds of miles away from my grandkids and be obedient to*

Scripture. I have to move. I have to do something different; I need to live close to them because I want to be obedient to this passage. As a result, we left a position of influence in ministry, and Diane and I moved to California for the primary purpose of living close to grandkids in this stage of our lives. Andrea's kids were teenagers, and we had been very close relationally and geographically when they were younger, and Ryan was just starting his family, so California became our destination.

I understood that I needed to teach my children *and* my grandchildren if I was to carry out the intent of what Scripture had to say.

Think four

The third theme is illustrated in this verse: "He commanded our forefathers [generation one] to teach their children [generation two], so the next generation would know them, even the children yet to be born [generation three], and they in turn would tell their children [generation four]" (Psalm 78:5–6 NIV1984).

Notice in this passage that there are two generations not yet born, so I must discipline myself to consider the *children* of the children not yet born. I have to be the right kind of grandfather to my grandchildren so they will be the same sort of intentional Christian grandparents to their grandchildren. We have to think four generations ahead.

2. Because of the incredible potential

Grandparents are second only to parents in their potential to influence children spiritually.

Grandparent, you are *second* in potential influence! You have more time with grandchildren than a Sunday school teacher, and a deeper relationship as well. You will influence them over a longer period than teachers or coaches, and you have wisdom. You are ideally positioned for deep spiritual impact in the lives of precious grandchildren. Grandparents and church leaders often overlook the significant truth that grandparents have more potential influence than children's workers, youth pastors, and Christian teachers.

Grandparents are ideally positioned for discipling. Think about these desirable factors in the discipler-disciplee interaction: (1) a close personal relationship, (2) long-term involvement, (3) knowledge of the strengths and weaknesses of the disciple, and (4) a discipler who is wise. These four factors put grandparents into the sweet spot of disciple-making.

From a national viewpoint, grandparents have the potential for significant influence due to the large number of grandparents in America. Depending on the source, there are approximately seventy-five to eighty million grandparents in the United States. I've estimated there may be as many as thirty million Christian grandparents in America by applying the percentage of individuals who profess to be a Christian as revealed by other surveys to the total number of grandparents.

The average grandparent has four to six grandchildren (depending on the source). That means that our "army" of thirty million grandparents has the potential to spiritually influence millions of children. We have incredible potential to impact. Let's get busy and do it!

3. Because of the eagerness of grandparents to have an impact

Grandparents are eager to be spiritual influencers of their grandchildren; in fact, they are more eager than some parents.

I have worked with a number of children's pastors to help them assess the impact of their ministry. One of the distressing factors that nearly every one of them faces is the infrequency of church attendance of children. The average child in most churches attends fewer than two times a month. I've asked many children's pastors to measure how many children under their care attend three times a month or more, and the numbers are staggering. In one large church with multiple services, it was fifty-two out of 1,263. In another, it was thirty-four out of 640, and in another, two out of 402 (yes, only two). In most, they had a child under their teaching for fifteen to eighteen hours *per year*. The average eight-year-old gets as much media time in two days as they get in church in one year.

Two groups defied the norm: the children of the workers themselves and a second group that was a surprise, children brought by grandparents. *Why would those children be much more regular in attendance?* I believe grandparents care more. I've noticed three reoccurring reasons:

1. Some of us didn't do so well in guiding our children spiritually as a parent, and grandchildren offer us a second chance. (My friend Tim Kimmel, author of *Extreme Grandparenting*, calls it the opportunity for a do-over, or a mulligan.)

2. Some are alarmed. Our adult children are not interested in Christianity, and we are afraid that our grandchildren won't follow Jesus. So we are committed to do everything we can, and that includes getting them to church each week.

3. Some of us care more because we are more aware that the end of life is closer and we want to make every moment count.

4. Because of the cultural deceit

The messages of culture go unchallenged when it comes to the role of grandparenting.

Our generation is bombarded with narcissistic messages to spend our retirement years enjoying life and focusing on ourselves. Dr. Josh Mulvihill will explore the cultural messages in greater depth in the next chapter, but for now I'll point out that the messages are contrary to the Bible's perspective.

Psalm 71:18 (NIV) eloquently describes the purpose for our later years: "Even when I am old and gray, do not forsake me, my God, till I declare your power to the next generation, your mighty acts to all who are to come." That ought to be the prayer of our hearts and our greatest desire.

On one occasion I invited a grandfather (Jim) to attend our national conference on grandparenting, and after an awkward couple of seconds, he rejected my invitation and said, "A conference on grandparenting? I don't really think I need that. I've got that down." I wondered afterward, *By whose standard does Jim have grandparenting down?* If he was grandparenting according to the cultural standard that says "love your grandchildren, help take care of them, and play with them," then I'm confident his assessment was correct. But did he "have grandparenting down" according to God's standard revealed in the Bible? I didn't know.

Church leaders must challenge culture's messages about grandparenting and help grandparents listen to Scripture's messages instead. Church leaders, this is essential to discipling our youngest generations.

5. Because we can do better

I've observed four types of Christian grandparents.

The biblical grandparent. These grandparents are far from perfect, but they understand the message of Scripture about their role in perpetuating faith to future generations. They are intentional; they seek to take advantage of every opportunity to influence spiritually. They play hard, love deeply, act crazy, and sacrifice often for their grandchildren. The biblical grandparent understands that these things are not the end, they are a means to an end so that they can develop a deep relationship with their grandsons and granddaughters that will impact them for eternity.

The cultural grandparent. Some Christian grandparents dearly love their grandchildren and show it by caring for them, doting on them, and spoiling them a little. They go to soccer games and school programs. They are amazing grandparents by cultural standards, but they have not thought about how they might have a spiritual influence. They have made the means the end, rather than keeping their focus on the greater purpose Scripture reveals.

The blocked grandparent. A grandma once stood to her feet as we were ending a teaching session and asked me, "But, Larry, what do I do? My son says I can either see my granddaughter or I can tell her about God. But I cannot do both, because the first time I mention God to her, I will not be allowed to see her again."

There are many grandparents who understand what Scripture says, but they can't act on it because of a barrier such as geographic distance, broken relationships, or divorce. Especially when adult children are indifferent to Christ, the barrier can seem insurmountable. Though some of the greatest heart pains of life come with these barriers, I have found that many grandparents are embarrassed to share their pain in a church setting. They feel alone and don't know what to do. They desperately need the encouragement and support that a church grandparenting ministry would bring.

The unequipped grandparent. Some grandparents have never explored the tools created to disciple children and grandchildren. They haven't thought of putting a children's Bible on the coffee table or learned how to address the cultural issues that grandchildren face. They don't know the apps for their phone that could be used to equip them for influence. The last two chapters in this book provide tools to equip you for the task of grandparenting.

We can do better. The *church* can do better. We can give the grandparent-grandchild relationship the attention it deserves. We can experience the joy of seeing grandparents in the cultural, blocked, or unequipped groups become biblical grandparents. As a result, thousands of children will be more effectively discipled, and we will see our faith perpetuated into future generations.

6. Because of the ministry vacuum

God began stirring me with a vision for a grandparenting focus, and my first step was to search for churches in America that had such a ministry. I found five or six churches that had done a one-time conference or class, but nothing ongoing. Google didn't know of one. I asked my ministry friends; they had never heard of such a ministry. I began to hear of names—but only a handful—that were focused on the grandparent-grandchild relationship. After a number of months, I found *one* grandparent ministry out of *thousands* of churches in the United States. How could something with so much significance be overlooked by so many? That's the reason we launched the Legacy Coalition.

When we started our ministry in 2016, the lack of attention given by churches to the grandparenting role was only one piece of the problem. There was a lack of resources on Christian grandparenting. Dr. Mulvihill found only seven books and one DVD series had been written since the year 2000. Most of those books were self-published, revealing that publishers didn't believe there was an audience. In addition, there was only one organization focused entirely on Christian grandparenting, The Christian

Grandparenting Network, led by one of my heroes, Cavin Harper.

The landscape has changed since 2016 and God is at work. Churches are launching grandparenting ministries and grandparents are becoming intentional about their role. Organizations are forming, and tools are being created. There is still much work to be done, and we believe you will want to be a part. Consider doing three things:

Join the movement.

Commit to becoming an *Intentional Christian Grandparent*.

Recognize in your church that *Grandparenting Matters* and consider starting a grandparent ministry.

Larry Fowler is the founder of the Legacy Coalition. His vision for a national grandparenting ministry brought together a gifted team of family, children's, and youth ministry leaders to launch this movement of God. His more than forty years of ministry include experience as a youth pastor, and as part of the Awana staff as missionary, training staff, international director, and executive leadership. He has extensive international experience, training children's workers in forty-seven countries, and has authored five books on children's and family ministry. He is a regular main-stage speaker and workshop presenter at conferences. In 2012 he was recognized for his lifetime of contribution to children's ministry in America by the International Network of Children's Ministry with their national Legacy Award. Larry and his wife, Diane, live in Riverside, California, and have two children and seven grandchildren.

2

Understanding the Biblical Role of Grandparents

BY JOSH MULVIHILL

What is the biblical role of a grandparent? Biblically, every member of the family has been given an important, God-ordained role that is not interchangeable with other members of the family. Husbands are told to be the head of the home and to lovingly lead their family (Ephesians 5:23). Wives are given the role of helpmate and are to follow their husband's servant leadership (Genesis 2:18; Ephesians 5:22). Children are told to honor their parents through obedience (Exodus 20:12; Ephesians 6:1).

If the Bible clearly defines the role of other family members, does it also define the role of grandparent?

I sought the answer to this question, which is summarized in this chapter. Additional reading on the subject is available in a multiyear PhD study in the books *Biblical Grandparenting* (for church leaders and deep readers) and *Grandparenting* (for casual readers). The Bible is clear on the role of a grandparent, but American culture is not, and many Christians have unintentionally adopted a non-biblical view of grandparenthood.

Cultural Messages about Grandparenting

In American culture there is great uncertainty concerning the meaning and purpose of old age. Ambiguity surrounds the grandparent role. For example, one author states that we have a "cultural crisis" concerning the meaning and purpose of old age. Another author states, "There is new uncertainty about what it means to be a grandparent and what grandparents are supposed to do." Many Christian grandparents do not understand their God-designed role or the specific ways God wants them to pass faith on to future generations.

America has created its own role for grandparents, known to scholars as "the new social contract." The core values of the social contract include non-interference by grandparents, emotional independence from children, and personal autonomy. Families unconsciously operate according to the agreement that children will grow up, move away, start their own family, and become independent from one another. Experts encourage families to aim for closeness at a distance, but that results in lonely, overburdened, and disconnected families. The social contract has amputated generations from one another and left countless grandchildren as grand-orphans who do not have the intimate influence of a grandparent in their life.

Because the role of grandparents is not clearly defined by American culture, it is viewed as an extra, a role not essential to the functioning of the family or the growth and development of grandchildren. Grandparents themselves fear meddling in their children's and grandchildren's lives. While the relationship, when it exists, can be very positive, its limited and tenuous nature removes grandparents from the central hub of family life and places them on the periphery with a minimal role.

Children's literature

Children's literature provides a glimpse into the role society assigns grandparents. A few notable titles include *Grandmas Are for Giving Tickles* and *Grandpas Are for Finding Worms*. The children's book *What Grandpas and Grandmas Do Best* suggests that grandparents are for playing hide-and-seek, singing a lullaby, building a sandcastle, and playing games. In *Grandma, Grandpa, and Me*, grandparents are to play with, work alongside, and have fun with. Children's literature speaks of a grandparent's role as one of playmate and companion.

The Villages

Andrew Blechman's book *Leisureville* captures the two primary roles of grandparents in American culture: independence and indulgence. *Leisureville* explores what life is like as a retired person living in the Villages, a gated community in Florida. The Villages is larger than Manhattan, boasts a population over 100,000, has a golf course for every day of the month, and has its own newspaper, radio, and TV station. The community is missing only one thing: children. The Villages not only encourages, but also legalized the segregation of ages from one another. No one under the age of nineteen may live there. Children may visit, but their stay is strictly limited to a total of thirty days a year. When Dave, one of the residents, was asked if he was uncomfortable living in a community without children, he answered, "I'm not thirteen. . . . I want to spend time with people who are my own age." Another resident says, "I raised my children and I didn't want to raise anyone else's."

The Villages sell a lifestyle that suggests retirees have worked hard, and now it is time to pursue hobbies, play golf, and socialize with peers. Instead of investing in future generations, older couples are encouraged to indulge themselves in travel, play, or whatever makes their retirement years enjoyable.

In general, society has lost its compass regarding why the generations should interact, how they are to do so, and what responsibilities one has to the other. Many Christian grandparents have embraced the *Leisureville* mentality and need a renewed biblical vision regarding their role in the family and purpose in society.

The Biblical Foundation for Grandparenting

The Bible has many references to grandparenting, but they are often missed because the Bible uses phrases such as children's children, son's son, father's father, or forefather to speak about grandparenting. As you read three examples, pay attention to the responsibilities God gives grandparents.

- "Teach them [God's commands] to your children and your *children's children*" (Deuteronomy 4:9 AMPC, emphasis added).
- "Fear the Lord your God, you and your son and your *son's son* by keeping all his statutes and his commandments, which I command you, all the days of your life, and that your days may be long. . . . You shall love the Lord your God with all your heart and with all your soul and with all your might. And these words that I command you today shall be on

your heart. You shall teach them diligently to your children" (Deuteronomy 6:2, 5–7, emphasis added).

- "Tell to the coming generation the glorious deeds of the Lord . . . which he commanded our *fathers* to teach to their children, that the next generation might know them, the *children yet unborn*" (Psalm 78:4–6, emphasis added).

The one word that describes the totality of a grandparent's role biblically is the word *heritage*. Grandparents have inherited a faith they are to pass on to their children (Ephesians 6:1–4; Deuteronomy 6:2–9) and their grandchildren (Deuteronomy 4:9; Psalm 78:1–8). This is the biblical idea of heritage.

Specifically, the grandparent's role is to be a disciple-maker of future generations by focusing on the salvation and sanctification of their family (Psalm 78:7–8). Grandparents are to pay close attention to their own walk with Christ (Deuteronomy 6:4) and live a Christ-centered life worthy of imitation so they can say to a grandchild, "Imitate me as I imitate Christ."

Psalm 78

Psalm 78 is one of my favorite passages to explain the role and responsibility God has given grandparents. Psalm 78 is a historical psalm that serves as a warning to motivate grandparents to look at a failed example of family discipleship in hopes of avoiding a similar outcome with their family. Psalm 78:8 states, "That they should not be like their fathers, a stubborn and rebellious generation, a generation whose heart was not steadfast, whose spirit was not faithful to God." The words *stubborn* and *rebellious* summarize the outcome this passage wants you to avoid with your family.

God identifies three key methods that are central to passing faith on to future generations (Psalm 78:1–7). First, God provides *a four-generation vision* for families: fathers, children, children yet unborn, and their children (Psalm 78:5–6). God wants you to think multigenerationally and gives you a large vision to leave a lasting legacy in Christ that will last for generations to come. We are here for a time we cannot see and are to live for a generation we may never meet.

The second aspect of a grandparent's role is to *tell God's works* and is found in Psalm 78:4: "Tell to the coming generation the glorious deeds of the Lord, and his might, and the wonders that he has done." To "tell" means to report, to count, to make known, to make a written record. God wants you to report to your grandchildren (the coming generation) what God has done in your life (His glorious deeds). Telling focuses on describing the work of God and His nature with the hope that your grandchildren will be captivated by God and worship Him. God has given you a testimony and wants you to be a messenger using your life as the means to glorify Him.

The third method is to *teach God's law* and is found in verse 5; God has "appointed a law in Israel, which he commanded our fathers [grandfathers or forefathers] to teach." Teaching is a central element of a grandparent's role. The Hebrew word *teach* means to instruct or guide. Guidance is a goal-oriented word. It suggests there is a specific outcome you are working toward, and teaching is a method to that end. A good guide knows the end destination, shows others the path, and instructs along the way.

Grandparents are to teach God's law, which includes the following:

- God is the source of morality. Your grandchild must develop the firm conviction that God determines right and wrong.

- The Gospel. Every grandchild has broken God's law and needs the free gift of grace through faith in Christ.

- Obedience to authority. Your grandchild must be encouraged to live in a manner worthy of the Gospel in accordance with God's commands (Matthew 28:18–20).

- The core truths of Christianity. The pattern of Scripture is for children of all ages to be taught the core truths of the Bible so that they will be firmly rooted in Christ and established in their faith (Colossians 2:7; 2 Timothy 1:5).

The overall aim of grandparenting is the salvation and sanctification of children and grandchildren. Psalm 78:7 speaks about this goal, "so that they should set their hope in God and keep his commands." God provides three methods to reach that goal: a multigenerational vision, telling His work through your testimony, and teaching obedience to God's commands based on the Bible.

Society communicates a powerful message that grandparents are extras, not essential to the family. Nothing could be further from the truth. If the history of Israel teaches us anything, it is that grandparents are critical figures in the faith formation of the young.

I want to encourage you to take your cues regarding the role of grandparenthood from the Bible and not from culture. A grandparent's main role is not to spoil a grandchild or be his or her companion. A grandparent's purpose is not to indulge themselves during the last third of their life. God designed grandparents as disciple-makers for the purpose of passing on a heritage of faith to future generations. May you pursue this task with much delight!

3

Starting a Legacy Grandparenting Ministry in Your Church

BY LARRY FOWLER

The concept of starting a grandparenting ministry is so new there are few models to build on. The Legacy Coalition has hundreds of years of combined expertise, and we believe there are six sequential elements that apply in most cases. With your help, we look forward to refining these steps and offering more ideas and resources to others who will follow in grandparenting ministry.

Step 1: Core Group

Any new ministry needs a group of people who are committed to its purpose and mission, and who are willing to lead. Of this group, it is likely none will be novices, so the following advice may not be necessary, but it is still helpful for them to think through each of the points below no matter how much experience they have.

How many leaders do we need? This depends on the size of your church; you will need more than two, but probably fewer than ten—even in a large church. Iron sharpens iron, so your core team will be more effective when there are multiple leaders. However, too large a group may actually slow it down.

Do they need to be grandparents? They will probably have more passion for the ministry if they are grandparents themselves. Along with being grandparents, they should also represent the variety of ages of the grandparents in your church; some should be young grandparents, and some with several years of experience as grandparents.

What do they need to know? They must be convinced of the biblical pattern of intergenerational discipleship. In other words, they must believe it is scriptural for grandparents to be intentional in providing spiritual influence to their grandchildren. A number of the materials in the Legacy Coalition Resource Kits provide a look at scriptural truth; the core group would do well to study this for themselves, so they are able to come to their own deep conviction about the necessity to focus on these truths.

They must believe in the need for grandparents to be equipped in their church; they must have a passion to activate and energize their peers. This will require the willingness to be vulnerable themselves, as being transparent about their own need to do better and to be more intentional will help them connect in deeper ways with the grandparents in their church.

What kind of giftedness do they need? Their gifts should be complementary; some may be more effective at communicating vision while others are gifted with organization and can structure the ministry efforts. The ability to communicate vision is huge, because it is likely other grandparents in the church may not be aware of their need to be more intentional. While the pastor-owner can do this too, it is critical for the grandparents in your church to be able to hear from their peers as well.

Step 2: Pastor-Owner

Let's face it: whether it is in a church with a single pastor or one with many staff members, launching a ministry is an uphill climb without a pastor "owning" the ministry. By owning, we mean there must be more than a pastor simply giving his blessing to the effort; he needs to have some skin in the game. He must feel some responsibility to support the core team and make this ministry launch a success. This doesn't necessarily mean a time commitment for him, but it does require his attention and a supporting attitude.

In a multiple-staff church, it may be the family pastor or the adult education pastor who "owns" the grandparenting ministry. If it is the family pastor, he will likely need to change his definition of family. In nearly all churches, "family pastor" means oversight of children's, youth, and parenting ministries; grandparents are simply not included. The definition of "family" must change from one that consists of a nuclear family to one that includes an extended family.

The pastor-owner must believe in the value and the potential of inter-generational ministry, and must see engagement of grandparents in the lives of their grandchildren as vital to carrying out this type of ministry.

The pastor-owner must be willing to have a vision beyond his own church, because many grandparents will have grandchildren in other churches, in other states, or not in church at all. He must be willing to equip them even if there is no direct benefit to the children in his church.

The pastor-owner will be responsible for aligning whatever is done for grandparents into the mission and vision of the church. He will make sure it reflects the DNA of the church, and provide encouragement or focus if the initial efforts of the core group fall short of expectations or flounder.

In a large church, the pastor-owner will represent the ministry to the rest of the pastoral staff, always seeking to bring cooperation and collaboration to the ministries that are involved.

Once you have identified your leadership, it is now time to register at legacycoalition.com! Let us know you are excited about the vision and will be developing this ministry in your church.

Go online to legacycoalition.com and register. Registering will greatly benefit us: we will be equipped through your registration to establish our national network of churches that catch the vision for intergenerational discipleship. But it will also benefit you, ensuring you are first to know about upcoming events, new resources, and ministry updates. We promise we won't deluge you with advertisements or email.

Step 3: Vision Event

What will the vision event be about? Vision for the discipleship role of a grandparent must be created from Scripture; therefore, there must be an opportunity to lead the grandparents in your church through a look at the biblical pattern for multigenerational involvement. Vision also involves unpacking the potential for spiritual influence in a grandparent-to-grandchild relationship. Nothing enhances a vision like personal stories; the core team members should be prepared to recount their own experiences as part of the vision event. Finally, a vision event will unpack the need for greater attention on this relationship. While this may sound complicated, it is really about sharing your heart for your grandchildren and how you really can impact them for Jesus. It is about sharing this vision with your church as a whole.

Who is the event for? Grandparents, of course! And you will want to structure it for maximum exposure to the grandparents in your church. Remember, your target audience includes all of them! If you do this with just the "senior saints" class, few of the younger grandparents will be able to come, as many of them still work, and others see the senior saints class as the one their parents attend. In fact, if you target one age range more than another, target the forty-five- to sixty-five-year-olds.

What does the vision event look like? Every church is different. Vision events should fit the culture of your church and opportunities that arise. Here are some possibilities:

A sermon series. Your pastor could take on the challenge of preaching a series of messages on the topic of intergenerational discipleship. A specific focus in this series should be the role of grandparents. "But what about all the younger adults in our congregation?" you ask. They also need this vision; it may help them in their interaction within their family structure and give them a vision for their future role as grandparents. If your pastor wants resources, several are listed in Step 5, but his own study of passages that speak to intergenerational relationships will strengthen his appreciation of this important topic! Two helpful resources we recommend are Cavin Harper's book, *Courageous Grandparenting*, and Dr. Josh Mulvihill's book *Grandparenting*.

A small group study, an adult Bible class study, or a grandparent's prayer group. This can begin with the core group, but the aim is to get the vision out to all the grandparents in the church. Therefore, offering just one small group on this topic won't do. We recommend Tim and Darcy Kimmel's video series, *Extreme Grandparenting*, or Legacy Coalition's *Grandparenting* DVD series. In addition, dozens of audios, and even videos from our national conference, the Legacy Grandparenting Summit, are available online for download at legacycoalition.com.

A seminar. Some of the initial videos in the series listed above work in a seminar format. If you would like a live presenter but don't know who to ask to lead a seminar, we can help. Many of the Legacy Coalition team are nationally recognized speakers and leaders, and may be available to come to your church to speak. In addition, we recommend Christian Grandparenting Network's Courageous Grandparenting seminar, Josh Mulvihill's Biblical Grandparenting seminar, or the Legacy Coalition's Grandparenting Matters seminar. Contact us at info@legacycoalition.com if you want to begin a conversation for a Grandparenting Matters seminar.

Step 4: Habit Change

We are talking first about habit change in your church: in order to have a vision for intentional spiritual grandparenting take root in your congregation, it must become a regular part of your church life. Just as you reference parenting frequently and seek to resource this relationship often, you must do the same with grandparenting. This is not a seasonal theme; neither is it another program; it is incorporating prayer for grandchildren, tips on grandparenting, biblical encouragement, and other things into the DNA of your church.

How can the topic of intentional Christian grandparenting be kept regularly in front of the grandparents in your church? The core team must not only answer this question, but also implement what they feel will work best. Think through some of these options:

- You could devote five minutes each week in the appropriate adult classes to pray for grandchildren (and adult children too).
- How about incorporating tips and/or encouragement in a newsletter or on a grandparenting Facebook page?

- Send home a weekly or monthly "table tent" with a specific prayer focus, questions a grandparent could ask their grandchildren to generate conversations, and information about upcoming events printed on it. Grandparents could put this on their table so they see and remember to use it each week or month. Or provide a link for grandparents to print their own.

As the legacycoalition.com web page grows, you will find many sources for articles, blogs, books, and videos. Check out our ministry partners as well, christiangrandparenting.net and grandsmatter.org. Their websites also contain many helpful resources. You'll be able to include reviews of products and resources in your emails and newsletters to the grandparents in your church that will be extremely helpful to them.

Your core team will need to meet regularly to discuss and pray for this ministry in order to keep the focus fresh and vibrant. Their vision for ongoing, regular ministry will fuel this and cause the ministry to grow.

Step 5: Equipping Opportunities

On a frequency basis of once a year to once a quarter, create a learning opportunity that equips grandparents. While the initial event will focus on the vision for an effective discipling relationship between grandparent and

...ndchild, future events would focus on equipping grandparents. This doesn't mean the scriptural foundation and other elements of vision are forgotten, however; they ought to be reviewed briefly in some way at every event.

Like the vision-casting event, these may be an adult class, a seminar, a small group study, or an organized opportunity to pray. If it fits your church's DNA, you may want to have "affinity groups" that are built around common needs or obstacles. You may want groups for single grandmas, those whose adult children have walked away from faith, or those who grandparent at a distance. This could be the way you arrange tables at your event or form small groups.

What about materials for this? We desire to see more become available, but for starters consider the following:

Courageous Grandparenting by Cavin Harper. A landmark book on grandparenting, this is a great foundation book on intentional grandparenting.

Biblical Grandparenting and *Grandparenting* by Dr. Josh Mulvihill. These books are one of a kind! *Biblical Grandparenting* is the only book in print that takes a research perspective of grandparenting and unpacks the biblical perspective, current Christian grandparents' attitudes toward grandparenting, and best practices.

- *Grandparenting Matters* **series** by Legacy Coalition authors. A series of short books that deal with common challenges grandparents face, such as being blocked by adult children, long-distance grandparenting, and prodigal family members.

- *Grandparenting: Loving Our Children's Children* by Phyllis and Andrew Le Peau. A great small-group tool, this book is part of InterVarsity Press's Life-Guide Bible Studies.

- *Grandparenting with a Purpose* by Lillian Penner. This book is focused on prayer and is a wonderful resource as that becomes a focus of your group.

- *Extreme Grandparenting* by Tim and Darcy Kimmel. An interactive video series complete with an accompanying text.

You may also want to meet needs based on the age of the grandchildren. While many grandparents have grandchildren across an age spectrum, the type of interaction is somewhat determined by the age of the grandchild. This is helpful if you want to have an equipping event that informs your group about the tools that may be used with grandchildren of various ages. Obviously, what you would recommend for preschool grandchildren will be quite different from what grandparents might use with teenagers.

Check out the Grandparenting Resource Kits that Legacy Coalition has assembled. We have saved you the challenge of shopping by selecting ten items for each age group—preschool, elementary, and teen—and including them in one kit. You can find these kits at legacycoalition.com.

Step 6: A Grand Activity

We recommend that once a year you hold a special event just for grandparents and their grandchildren. The purpose of this event is to celebrate the grandparent-grandchild relationship and provide an opportunity for them to create a special memory.

Encourage the grandparents in your church to invite out-of-town grandchildren or "adopt" a grandchild who does not have a grandparent nearby for the day. Or you could work through the children's and youth ministries and encourage your church children and youth to invite their grandparents, in town or out, to this event as well.

What might you do for the day? Have fun! Create some memories! Use your creativity! You could:

- Celebrate the end of school and start of summer with a picnic in the park!
- Celebrate the start of school with an opportunity to serve together as you gather and pack back-to-school

supplies for children in your community who are in need, and then enjoy popcorn and watch a family movie together!

- Plan a time to bake cookies for Christmas—have each family bring their favorite recipe printed to share and the ingredients to bake a couple dozen. Share cookies and swap recipes. Take lots of photos! Finish the evening with a time to go Christmas caroling to shut-ins and share some cookies with them too!

These are just a few of the ways you can provide opportunities for grandparents and grandchildren to connect, build their relationships, and have fun together! As the legacycoalition.com website grows, you will want to post what you do for your special activity, and learn from others who do the same.

You may choose to do it as a one-day event. However, if you want to have an experience even more meaningful, seek out a campground where a GrandCamp weekend is being held. Check out the tab on the christiangrandparenting.net website that is devoted to this event. More and more Christian campgrounds are realizing the ministry potential for this event and are planning getaways.

Whatever you choose, provide an opportunity for grandparents and grandchildren to connect, build their relationships, and have purposeful fun together!

4

Helping Your Church Become More Intergenerational

BY WAYNE RICE

Emma Unruh had a huge influence on me when I was a child. She was an elderly lady in our church who always sat on the front pew and would "get happy" during the singing of hymns or the saying of prayers. She would wave her handkerchief in the air and shout, "Hallelujah! Praise the Lord!" During the sermon, she would let out an "Amen!" or "Yes!" which I know helped our pastor preach better than he could have otherwise. Mrs. Unruh did this sort of thing every week and I loved it. She made me smile. She made me want to have the same kind of joy in my heart. She made me want to know Jesus the way she knew Him.

I was blessed to have a number of people like Mrs. Unruh in my life when I was growing up. They were all right there, Sunday morning, Sunday night, and Wednesday night prayer meeting. I heard them give their testimonies, pray, and sing the old hymns. I sat under their teaching, visited their homes, ate at their tables, laughed at their stories, and cried at their funerals. They were all saints to me and I will never forget them.

The church I grew up in was an intergenerational church.

You don't find many churches like that anymore—where old folks and young people worship together, sing together, pray together, eat green Jell-O at church potlucks together, serve and follow Jesus together.

More likely, you'll find churches that divide the congregation by age. Families may come to church in the same car, but upon arrival, they head off in several different directions—to the nursery, the children's ministry, the middle school ministry, the high school ministry, the college or young adult ministry, the adult worship service, or the senior or "traditional" service.

Bringing the Church Together Again

Research confirms that grandparents rank second only to parents when it comes to spiritual influence on children. One of the reasons grandparents rank so high is because they usually get to spend more time with their grandchildren than anyone else besides their parents. And children naturally gravitate to the oldest people they can find who will pay attention to them, listen to them, and encourage them. In order to be that kind of person, you have to be with them.

Churches are families by definition (Hebrews 2:11). The older members of the congregation can be like grandparents to the children of the church. The potential for spiritual influence is huge. But in order for that to happen, there must be opportunities for the church family to be together on a regular basis. The church has to become more intergenerational.

For five years I served College Avenue Baptist Church in San Diego as pastor to generations. During that time, we began transitioning from being an age-segregated church to becoming an intergenerational church. The process is ongoing, but here are some of the things we were able to accomplish:

We unified our Sunday morning worship services. We did away with services catering to particular age groups and personal preferences. Now we have one unified service where everybody worships together, from children through senior adults. We are still learning how to worship together—all ages at the same time, in the same space, with the same order of worship, the same music, the same sermon. It's not easy, but we are learning humility and learning that worship is not about what I like, but what God likes. And surely God likes it when His church worships together in unity (Psalm 133:1).

We hold an all-church retreat every year. During the winter or early spring, we hold an all-church weekend retreat for all ages. The theme is usually community-building, and a highlight of the weekend is our church's annual amateur talent and variety show.

We started a mentoring program to intentionally connect older members of the congregation with young people. At one of our church retreats, I conducted a "speed mentoring" experience, similar to speed dating. Two concentric circles of chairs (facing each other) were formed. Older folks were on the outer circle, young people on the inner circle. Each young person had a list of questions to ask the older person. After five minutes, conversations stopped and the inner circle moved one or two chairs to the left (or right). Some of our young people commented that this was the best part of the entire church retreat.

We conduct intergenerational mission trips every summer. We no longer conduct high school mission trips, junior high mission trips, college mission trips, adult-only mission trips. Instead, we conduct intergenerational mission trips so that young and old alike can experience missions together. It's a wonderful thing when children, parents, and grandparents all serve Christ together. That's how faith gets passed on from one generation to the next!

We began an all-church Christmas party. In the past, almost every age group of the church held its own Christmas party, sometimes competing with each other for decorations, food service, entertainment, and space. So we decided to combine all those Christmas parties into one big "Christmas Extravaganza," and the result has been an evening of celebration that is sure to become a wonderful memory for our children and grandchildren.

Of course, there will always be times when it's necessary or more appropriate for children, youth, young adults, middle-agers, and older adults to do things with their own age groups. But every church can become more intergenerational by simply asking, "How can we bring people together more often rather than dividing them up?" If you are a church leader, then cast the vision, get a few people on your team, brainstorm ideas together, and experiment. It's unlikely you will have to make big changes at first. Just add an intergenerational component to some of the programs and activities that already exist. If you are having a social activity for the senior adults, invite the youth group. If you are planning a service project for the youth group, invite some of the seniors. You'll be amazed by what happens when young and old spend a little time together.

We really do want our churches to be the family of God in more than just words. Grandparents and parents alike have to be intentional about spending quality time with their children. Likewise, the family of God has to be intentional as well. I have worked with youth groups most of my adult life and I always love to tell teenagers, "I want to introduce you to some grandmas, grandpas, uncles, and aunts you never knew you had. . . . It's called the church!"

Wayne Rice has been active in youth ministry, family ministry, and grandparenting ministry for more than fifty years. He is the co-founder of Youth Specialties, creator of Understanding Your Teenager seminars, former pastor to generations at College Avenue Baptist Church in San Diego, and currently the director of conferencing for the Legacy Coalition. Wayne has authored dozens of books including *Junior High Ministry*, *Reinventing Youth Ministry [Again]*, *Generation to Generation*, and *Engaging Parents as Allies in Youth Ministry*. He received the Gold Medallion award from the Evangelical Christian Publishers Association (ECPA) for his book *Up Close and Personal: Building Community in Youth Groups*. Wayne and his wife, Marci, live in Alpine, California. They have three grown children and five grandchildren. Wayne also plays the banjo.

5

An Intergenerational Grandparenting Ministry Model

First Evangelical Free Church in Fullerton, California

BY JOHN COULOMBE

How do you develop a purposeful, effective, vibrant, Christ-centered ministry to grandparents in your church and community? This chapter addresses some lessons we have learned and mistakes we have made as we developed a grandparenting ministry in Fullerton. As I share our model, please remember that one size does not fit all, especially as it relates to churches.

I came to EvFree Fullerton in California to be the pastor to senior adults, or as we sometimes call them, experienced adults. I served in my pastoral role to seniors for many years, then our church culture changed when our senior adults "came of age" and a "new old" joined the ministry. As a result, we realized we needed to adapt our focus in order to reach the next generation.

I knew we needed to make some changes. But what to do? What was the issue? The boomer culture of my church resisted becoming a new senior group. They didn't want to be a group with lots of events or long-term commitments. Time had become more valuable as the world began to turn faster and priorities were changing.

We learned that potlucks and bus trips were not the answer. Instead, they wanted to experience life, climb mountains, and make a difference in the world. They wanted to live on the edge and be more mission-minded. They longed for meaningful moments with their grandchildren and children.

We wondered how we could challenge them to give the best of their time, talent, and treasure to God. I wanted to help those I pastored leave an eternal legacy to their offspring, not just temporary treasures. I wondered how to impact them with the things of the Lord that are eternal.

Find a New Focus

Our first step in beginning a grandparent ministry was a new ministry focus. I presented a new job description and direction for ministry to our newly appointed senior pastor. He listed some of his core values when he came, one being intergenerational ministry. I also presented a new job title to become the interGen pastor. I proposed that I would continue to minister to the oldest among us but would like to end the segregation and isolation of the age groups and attempt to bring the hearts of the generations together.

Our mantra became *Better Together Than Alone*. I suggested we would not plan more age-siloed programs but bring all age groups together so they could become acquainted. Instead of the high school students serving the older adults, what if both groups served together, ate together, and shared life together. And so we began the new journey—together.

God refined my ministry focus again when my wife, Jacque, and I had lunch with Larry and Diane Fowler. As we listened to Larry's grandparenting vision, it clicked. That vision was the answer to two big questions: *How do I encourage ongoing discipleship with older adults? How do we move from the aging issues to more important matters—their relationship with Christ and with their children and grandchildren*?

What if the focus was no longer on age, health, personal needs, desires, a changing church, or the worship music, but rather on the most important things, like our relationship with the Lord, family, children, grandchildren, neighbors, and our world? Instead of only focusing on our own age group, we now concentrated on our relationship with the Lord and the most significant people in our lives—our children and grandchildren. Our new focus changed our attitudes and turned our world upside down!

Select Leaders

We slowly refocused our energy on selecting people of like mind, heart, and purpose—leaders with a variety of gifts, backgrounds, and experiences. Most important, we chose individuals committed to God and His Word, struggling themselves with the brokenness in their own lives and families yet vulnerable, open, and growing. We highly value the power of prayer as we discern God's direction for this fledgling ministry.

We have gradually, prayerfully, collectively been designing the program as we go. As Larry stressed, recruiting the right people for the right ministry roles is vital. After selecting leaders with similar conviction, passion, and vision, here's how we began.

Host an Introductory Event

To introduce our grandparenting ministry, we created a five-week course on Sunday mornings following worship services entitled Equip-U. We served lunch and included fun crowdbreakers around the tables that focused on the "grand" folks in their lives, with short but informative teachings on grandparenting. Our teaching methods included video, speakers, panel discussion, Q&A, and testimonies.

The five sessions included:

1. Catch a vision for grandparenting.
2. What does Scripture say about grandparenting?
3. Barriers, challenges, and opportunities to grandparenting.
4. Ideas and a how-to session with a panel.
5. *The Blessing* teaching, concluding with a short celebration and dedication service.

Provide a Quarterly Gathering

We scheduled a quarterly gathering on a Thursday evening for our Grandparenting Huddles, which include a training session on subjects like long-distance grandparenting, *The Blessing*, how to teach grandchildren wisdom and truth, the hows and whys of praying for grandchildren, and the barriers and bridges in family relationships.

At the end of each session we spend time praying for our children and grandchildren. When we honestly and authentically open up and come together with other grandparents with broken hearts and humility, God answers! When we entrust ourselves to others with those kind of raw petitions, we often have praises to share next time we gather at a Grandparent Huddle. It is energizing to see God at work in both our lives and our loved ones'.

Offer Annual Events

Besides the quarterly Grandparent Huddles for training, support, and prayer, we offer two annual intergenerational events that bring grandchildren and grandparents together. We call them Grand Day Out or Grand Break-Away! We have two different events: one for younger grandchildren and a separate event for older grandchildren due to the difference of interests and needs for different ages.

An example of a Grand Day Out is an early Saturday tide-pool trip to the beach to watch the sun come up, enjoy breakfast together, and learn about God's wisdom, goodness, and the gift of creation! In the summer we plan a Youth Safari for older grandchildren where we shoot archery, BB guns, and skeet; learn gun safety, trick horseback riding, and falconry; go kayaking and rock climbing;

watch hunting dogs at work; and learn to make hooks for fly-fishing.

We encourage all our grandparents to be involved in summer Vacation Bible School, helping out in their grandchild's class and bringing them home that week to follow up with what they are learning each day. For ten summers Jacque and I have led a three-day Camp Grammy and Papa at our home with our eight grandchildren.

Adopt Spiritual Grandchildren

What about individuals who have never married or do not have grandchildren? Are they to be excluded from the task of passing on their faith in Christ and their God-stories to another generation? No! We have several unmarried individuals on our team who have taken on the task of being a voice to their nieces, nephews, and younger children of their friends whom they have chosen to adopt as spiritual grandchildren.

Due to the mobility of families, many grandchildren lack an intimate relationship with their grandparents and are church orphans with no spiritual mentor. We encourage individuals to consider spiritually adopting a grandchild.

Consider Starting a Grandparenting Ministry

A grandparenting ministry is one of the best ways to challenge older saints to grow in their walk with Christ and make a difference in their home, church, and world. Grandparenting is great motivation to stay in the race and finish well. The most important legacy we can leave behind is children and grandchildren who love, follow, serve, and share Christ. As the family goes, so goes the church. Maybe that's why the church has struggled to carry out the Great Commission. There is no better way to reach a needy world than beginning at home.

A grandparenting ministry can help toward these ends. There's nothing as motivating as young eyes watching Grammy and Papa live out their faith. And then there are the eyes of our grown children who know us oh so well. May they see Jesus alive, working in and through our lives, our walk, and our talk.

For those of us struggling with past failure, family conflicts, friction, and broken relationships, this can be a starting place where humility, forgiveness, renewal, and reconciliation can begin—and a restored relationship with the Lord! That's discipleship and spiritual reformation at its best!

John Coulombe is the interGen pastor at First Evangelical Free Church in Fullerton, California, where he has served for the past thirty years. John has served over the past fifty years as pastor to youth, families, senior adults, and currently as interGen pastor overseeing boomer and "Experienced Adults" ministries. Over the years he has helped establish Travel Camping with both the young and old along with *Ecclesia* (Community Pastors' Fellowship in Santa Barbara), *CASA International* (Christian Association of Senior Adults), and *Desert and Music-City Fathers* (annual encouragement/support retreats with ministry brothers and their friends). John is a founding member of the Legacy Coalition where he serves as director of connecting. He and his childhood sweetheart, Jacque, recently celebrated fifty years of marriage and are intentional in passing their faith and hope on to their eight grandchildren. John and Jacque also have two sons and daughters-in-love!

6

Ten Steps to Begin a Grandparent Ministry

BY JOANNE LUNDBERG

If you are like me, you are reading this book because you are exploring the possibility of beginning a ministry to grandparents. If there are millions of Christian grandparents in America, shouldn't churches be mobilizing, resourcing, and equipping us?

Who are the grandparents in your church? On one end of the spectrum are grandparents who are trying to influence their grandchildren with the Gospel. They are active and use every means to encourage grandchildren in their spiritual growth. On the other end of the spectrum are grandparents who have fallen into the fun factor and baby-sitter role with no thought to intentionally contributing to the spiritual growth of grandchildren. In addition, there are grandparent-aged adults who have the opportunity to influence neighborhood children, nieces, and nephews. Every one of these individuals would benefit from the shepherding guidance of their local church.

My Journey

The Lord squeezed on my heart at the first Legacy Grandparent Summit in 2016 where I gained a vision for biblical grandparenting. For a year, I talked to everyone who would listen and was convinced that we needed a grandparent ministry at our church. I asked the Lord to impress the need on a leader in our midst.

God answered my prayer in an unexpected way. Holly Miller, the director of Children and Family Ministries, invited me to consider a new position as a part-time staff member to begin a grandparent ministry. After talking with my family and praying, I felt the Lord was affirming this new direction. My new role is the Grandparent Ministry lead, and we believe that I may be the first individual brought on paid staff by a church to specifically equip grandparents to disciple future generations.

———— How Did I Begin a Grandparent Ministry? ————

Step 1: I solicited a prayer warrior or two to bring this ministry effort before the throne of God. My greatest hurdle was the fear of not being able to succeed. I admitted my fear to a couple of friends and asked them to join me in prayer.

Step 2: I invited grandparents to our home for a couple of meetings. The purpose was to cast the vision and to find a core group of committed grandparents who also saw a need for this ministry and who might be interested in committing time to exploring this together. We spent time praying for the ministry and spreading the word to others.

Step 3: I identified all the grandparents in the church and created a database with email addresses. I accomplished this task with the help of adult Sunday school classes.

Step 4: I sent out a mass email to those in the database announcing the start of the ministry and inviting them to our fall volunteer ministry training, which is when we launched our grandparent ministry. We asked Josh Mulvihill if he would train the volunteers and grandparents. When the children's ministry volunteers separated into department meetings, we assembled as grandparents. Josh spoke about the biblical mandate for grandparenting and the important role of teaching God's truth and telling the wonderful works of God to our children's children. Twenty-seven grandparents attended! They were very enthusiastic and encouraging, which revealed that there was an interest and a need.

Step 5: I made announcements about the new grandparent ministry and its role at New Hope Church in our adult Sunday school classes.

Step 6: I showed the Legacy Grandparent DVD series at our first gatherings. I wanted interested grandparents to be as excited as I was! I showed the same DVD twice in a week; once in the morning and on a different day in the evening. I used a different DVD every other week for a couple of months and then once a month to generate momentum. We spent approximately thirty minutes in table discussions after each video. Momentum was slow, but gradually more grandparents were catching the vision.

Step 7: I partnered with the family ministries team to include grandparents in events that were already on the church calendar for families. We encouraged grandparents to invite their grandchildren to join them at all-church events. Our goal is to facilitate opportunities for grandparents to have special connect time with their grandchildren by strategically utilizing our Fall Family Fun Fair, the Family Advent event, the Family Easter event, and New Hope Serves—the day our church body serves our community.

Step 8: I had communication tools created by working with our church staff to print a postcard and a poster with our name, purpose, and my contact information for questions. We posted announcements on Facebook and church monitors as well as distributed the postcards and posters around the church.

We listed Grandparent Ministry on our webpage with my contact information. We created a Legacy group page on the church website with our calendar of events and documents with resources for grandparents. The documents include teaching topics and notes, a list of online resources, book lists, activity ideas list, great gifts ideas, a list of baby equipment and toys that can be borrowed from each other for visiting grandchildren, and a list of blessings from the Bible and other sources to help grandparents begin the habit of reciting blessings over their grandchildren.

Step 9: I created a grandparenting library by gathering resources that can be checked out, used, and returned for others to use. I purchased the books listed in the last two chapters of this book.

Step 10: We are planning grandparent and grandchild prayer times in partnership with the youth ministry. Grandparent-aged adults will join the youth program one evening for a time of fellowship. Grandparents are encouraged to sign up as a prayer partner to one of the teens from our church youth group.

We are planning one-time events focused on interactive teaching with grandparents and their grandchildren, such as a creation science day with a creation science teacher, learning a skill or hobby, a service project day, and how to teach a Bible topic like "the armor of God" in a fun and interactive way.

Equipping Grandparents

There is one thing that could have stopped me from taking the opportunity offered me by New Hope Church and that was fear that I would fail or that there would be no interest. The Lord addressed that for me in this verse: "God did not give us a Spirit of fear but of power and love and self-control" (2 Timothy 1:7 NET). We are servants. The real leader is Christ. It is His ministry! Submit to the work of the Holy Spirit and His Word.

Should your church mobilize, resource, and equip grandparents? The answer is yes. It may not look like New Hope Church. Whatever shape it takes, grandparents should be encouraged and equipped to be disciple-makers of future generations.

Joanne Lundberg has been married to her husband, Dan, for forty-three years! They have three married children and five grandchildren. She homeschooled two of her children. When she sent the youngest to college, she began her twenty-four-year career in children's ministry at New Hope Church in Minnesota. After retiring, she stayed on at New Hope Church to begin a Grandparent Ministry for that congregation and feels that everything she's done before prepared her for this vital ministry!

7

Casting the Vision to Your Pastor

BY SHERRY SCHUMANN

Do you have grandchildren and understand the vital importance of cultivating their faith? Do you believe you can actively take part in discipling your grandchildren? Do you have a passion to grandparent with a purpose, but wonder where, when, and how to begin? If so, consider the following six steps to help you cast the vision for a grandparenting ministry to the pastor at your church.

1. Pray!
2. Begin a conversation by scheduling an appointment with your pastor.
3. Cast a compelling vision.
4. Provide a specific ask.

5. Be the grandparent champion at your church.

6. Leave the results up to God.

Step 1: Pray!

If you feel burdened to see grandparents purposefully engaged in training their grandchildren to cultivate godliness and a life that brings glory to Christ, then your first step is easy: Pray about it. Ask God to prepare the heart of your pastor and to give you the wisdom to share the vision with him. The best place to begin is to take time to ask God to go before you!

Step 2: Schedule a Conversation with Your Pastor

This step is also easy. Schedule an appointment with your pastor to start the conversation. A pastor's schedule is often full, and to ensure you can cast your vision for a grandparent ministry with limited distractions, carve out a specific time and place to meet. Don't forget to show respect by being on time.

Step 3: Cast a Compelling Vision

It is critical for you to cast a concise but compelling vision. Spend time organizing your vision; perhaps create an outline. Offer several reasons why a grandparent ministry is vital to the spiritual life of future generations. Provide biblical support by explaining to your pastor how Scripture mandates we tell the next generations the commandments, praiseworthy deeds, and wonders of the Lord (Psalm 78:4–6; Deuteronomy 4:9, 6:1–2; Psalm 145:4).

Step 4: Be Specific

When casting your vision to a pastor, it may be helpful to offer specific resources that will help train, equip, and empower grandparents to pass a spiritual legacy to future generations. Additionally, realize a grandparenting ministry is customizable, depending on your church size, demographic make-up, and available resources. For instance, you may ask your pastor to lead the effort in forming a grandparenting ministry, or you may ask for the pastor's blessing on your efforts to lead. Perhaps you want to ask for resources, such as books and conferences. Whatever you decide, be specific when you meet with your pastor to let him know what you desire the grandparenting ministry to look like in your church, and be open to the pastor's input when it comes to customizing your vision to fit the needs of the church.

Step 5: Be the Grandparent Champion at Your Church

Consider yourself a grandparent champion, a liaison between the pastor and those leading the grandparenting ministry or those leading the grandparenting ministry and the grandparents in your church. In addition, find simple ways to champion your vision of purposeful grandparenting by frequently praying over the grandparents in the church, giving announcements about upcoming conferences or small group studies on grandparenting, or making available resources that train and equip grandparents.

Step 6: Leave the Results Up to God

Trust God for the results. Ask Him to spread the vision to the pastoral staff and congregation. Know you cannot force a vision on others, but you can enthusiastically share and model purposeful grandparenting.

Sherry Schumann is a retired math and science teacher, a charter member of Legacy Coalition, and serves as the prayer coordinator for Christian Grandparenting Network. She delights audiences with bits and pieces of her own redemption story as she delivers a powerful message about prayer. Sherry and her husband of thirty-five years reside in Moncks

Corner, South Carolina, with their English setter named Finley. They treasure spending time with their three sons, three daughters-in-love, and four precious grandchildren. Sherry's novel, *The Christmas Bracelet*, makes readers laugh and cry, sometimes simultaneously.

8

Seriously, Another Program?
What Does Grandparenting Ministry
Really Mean for Pastors?

BY CAVIN HARPER

Two weeks after my twenty-second birthday I became a parent, but I had no idea what it meant to be a parent or what I was supposed to do. However, I knew where to turn, because my church and parachurch organizations like Focus on the Family offered plenty of resources to help me learn and figure it all out.

Years later, when I became a grandparent, I found myself faced with a similar question: What is this grandparenting thing all about? I knew I was going to enjoy being a grandfather, but I didn't have a clue what I was supposed to do beyond spoiling my grandchildren and sending them home to Mom and Dad to deal with. This time, however, when it came to finding resources and help, there were none to be found. I didn't know of any churches with classes about grandparenting and I was unable to find a single family ministry in America that spoke to the role of grandparents.

Grandparents today are pretty much in the same place I was when I first became a grandparent; they still wonder what they are supposed to do, except now there are ministries to help!

A Resource for Grandparents

I recently sat down with the leader of a regional denominational group of churches to discuss the biblical vision for grandparenting—how grandparents matter to God and how they need to matter to the Church. He agreed, but as we talked he raised concerns about another program being added to all the plates he was already trying to keep spinning. He also expressed how this would impact the pastors and church staff under his care with their already full plates.

I can identify with this pastor. I served on a pastoral staff for more than seventeen years and understand the pressure from outside groups wanting us to jump on the bandwagon with the latest trend in church ministry. This denominational leader's concerns were well founded, but I assured him that we have no desire to add another program to his already full to-do list. Our vision for an effective grandparenting ministry does not involve creating another program, but instead is focused upon expanding our understanding of family. As we spoke, I could see him relax and breathe a deep sigh of relief.

If you, like this church leader, think of your role as building and maintaining "programs," then it is understandable how this new ministry target group of grandparents might create some angst. We are talking, after all, about the Youth For Christ Alumni generation—the boomers. Youth ministry was built around this generation, and now here they come again, right?

A Radically Altered Way of Thinking about Family

When it comes to grandparenting ministry, we are proposing a different path, because if you think program, it's likely the whole point of equipping grandparents will be lost. Hit the DELETE button and step back from the mindset that drives other programs. Instead, embrace an entirely different way—a more biblical way, we believe—of thinking about grandparenting ministry.

The key difference is a radically altered way of thinking about family. It is a call to reject the deconstructed definition of family that essentially restricts the definition to the nuclear family. Instead, we believe we must move toward a reconstructed biblical model where family is defined as the entire multigenerational extended family. In this definition each generation has a significant part to play in the spiritual formation of the other, especially the older generations with the youngest generations.

Why is this shift important? Three reasons:

Changing how we think about family expands the conversation beyond just parents when we talk about teaching and discipling the next generations. The nuclear family model has excluded grandparents and other family members from consideration in the equation as significant spiritual influencers of our children. Yet the truth is, grandparents are second *only* to parents as the greatest potential influencers of a child in matters of spiritual formation.

A shift in our view of family means we don't have to build a new program targeting grandparents. We can now address grandparents at the same time we address parents. While roles will be distinctive, the foundational principles apply to both. It also allows us to address ways to help parents and grandparents work as allies, not adversaries.

If we don't embrace this, then we risk having an entire generation lost to the Gospel. The grandchildren of Joshua and Caleb's generation grew up not knowing the Lord and the amazing things He had done in Israel. We too risk losing our grandchildren to the enemy who will gladly steal their hearts and minds away from the truth.

What does this look like in practical terms for pastors?

Pastoral oversight remains focused on making sure the processes that will be used to prepare both parents and grandparents to fulfill their roles well is biblically sound and effective. They don't have to figure out how to staff another program model.

With this approach, pastors and other church staff can concentrate on the biblical teaching and training of family members under one umbrella—family ministry. Pastoral staff now focus their energies on using existing programs with an expanded audience.

Nothing has to be created from scratch. Sufficient high-quality resources and assistance are available to help church staff develop an effective, biblically sound approach to your role of teaching and equipping both parents and grandparents. Several good resources are available. Many more are already being developed to assist you.

As you reconstruct your thinking and approach to family ministry, imagine the enormous benefit in your church. More families will be healthier and stronger. Children will grow up learning what it means to walk in the truth and follow Christ because they are learning it at home, not just in church. These children who are being taught by parents and grandparents are more likely to remain involved in the local church body as adults.

The Christian Grandparenting Network stands ready to serve you and to help you launch a ministry focus that engages what you already have in place to expand your equipping role, so both parents and grandparents will impact the next generations for Christ—generations that will know, love, and serve Christ with all their hearts.

Cavin Harper is the founder and president of the Christian Grandparenting Network and the author of *Courageous Grandparenting*, *Living Your Will*, *A GrandCamp Field Guide*, and *Wayfinder* (a novel). He and his wife, Diane, are the creators of GrandCamps, now in its twentieth year. He writes a weekly blog, hosts a grandparenting podcast called *Family Impact*, and travels as a speaker and presenter of Courageous Grandparenting seminars and workshops in churches throughout the United States and Canada. Cavin and Diane were married in 1969 and have two daughters and nine grandchildren. Their home is in Colorado Springs.

9

Eight How-to Resources for Grandparents

BY LYNDA FREEMAN

Do you remember the day you learned you were going to become a grandparent for the first time? What did you think? Were you certain you must be too young to be a grandparent? Did you feel excited?

What about the first time you saw your sweet grandchild? Did you marvel at how small they were? Were you surprised by their bald head, or all their hair! When you held them and looked into those little eyes, what did you think? Was your heart practically bursting with love? Did you wonder, *What do I do now? What kind of grandparent will I be?*

You may have had grandparents who were very engaged with you and who knew how to pass on a heritage of faith, or maybe you did not and are wondering how to do this. Babies do not come with an instruction book for parents, and they do not come with one for grandparents either.

However, God's Word does tell us much about being a grandparent. I could fill this article with passages from God's Word about grandparenting, but will just share one of my favorite passages, which tells me what I am supposed to be doing as a grandma.

> As a father has compassion on his children,
>   so the Lord has compassion on those who fear him;
> for he knows how we are formed,
>   he remembers that we are dust.
> The life of mortals is like grass,
>   they flourish like a flower of the field;
> the wind blows over it and it is gone,
>   and its place remembers it no more.
> But from everlasting to everlasting
>   the Lord's love is with those who fear him,
>   and his righteousness with their children's
>   children—
> with those who keep his covenant
>   and remember to obey his precepts.
>
> Psalm 103:13–18 NIV

I *love* this passage! It reminds me of several important facts that I want my grandchildren to know and believe with all their hearts! Take a look at them:

God has compassion on me.

God knows how I was formed—

He remembers I am just a person.

He knows my life is short.

His love for me has no end.

His love is not just for me, it is for my children's children too!

Remembering and obeying God matters.

So from these verses I know that just as God shows compassion to me and remembers I am just a person, I will do the same with my grandchildren. I will show them compassion. I will not expect perfection from them. I will give them grace because I love them! Most important, I will be sure they know how very much God loves them—that God's love is for them! And we will talk often about how much it matters that we obey and remember God and all He does for us.

Knowing these things are all true helps me know what I need to be doing as a grandma. They are my "how-tos."

Yes, God's Word is our "go-to" for all of our "how-do-I" questions, but I'm very happy to say there are also a number of excellent books available that we can use as well. Here are eight of them.

Eight Books for Grandparents

Extreme Grandparenting by Tim and Darcy Kimmel
Grandparents have a vital role in the lives of their grandchildren, not only as mentors and loving family members, but as spiritual rocks in hard times. *Extreme Grandparenting* helps readers understand how to make the most of the new role of grandparent and how to grow the next generation for greatness.

Great Lessons & Grand Blessings by Elmer and Ruth Towns
As a grandparent, you have once again experienced the miracle of new life in your family. Being a grandparent means you are older, wiser, and you can offer your grandchildren something invaluable: the gift of influencing them for Christ. In *Great Lessons & Grand Blessings*, Elmer and Ruth Towns will take you on a journey through the lives of famous—and infamous—grandparents of the Bible. By studying the lives of biblical grandparents, you will learn some of God's greatest lessons and grandest blessings— even if you believe you have failed in the past.

Courageous Grandparenting by Cavin Harper
This book is a call for grandparents and parents to rise above the conventional view of grandparenting to embrace a radically courageous life that stands

apart from the politically correct crowd. *Courageous Grandparenting* is a call to intentionality—not settling for simply being good parents and grandparents, but choosing to stand in the gap and live as conduits of grace and truth for the next generations. There is too much at stake not to.

Deeper In 4 Grandparents & Parents, Too! Praying the Scriptures for the Children You Love by Lynda Freeman

When you look at the world around you, do you wonder how your children and grandchildren will grow up to love, know, and follow God with faithful hearts? There are so many things to deceive them and sidetrack or derail their walk with God. But we do not have to wonder or worry. We can pray and know that God not only hears our prayers, but He also listens and answers them as well! With *Deeper in 4 Grandparents & Parents, Too!* you will find fifty-two weeks of Scripture prayers from the Old Testament or Psalms, which guide you in praying specifically for God's Word to be shown in your own life and the lives of the children you love! This focus on praying God's Word for yourself and your grandchildren and children will give you the opportunity to do something that makes a difference: pray!

Biblical Grandparenting and *Grandparenting* by Josh Mulvihill

What is the role of a grandparent? While the world tells you it is time to retire and relax, you have the opportunity to make a difference in the lives of your grandchildren and leave a lasting heritage for your family. These books explain culture's misleading messages about grandparenting, provide a biblical overview of the role of grandparents, share groundbreaking research that will give you a vision to impact the next generation for Christ, and offer practical methods to disciple your grandchildren and navigate family challenges. *Biblical Grandparenting* is based on Josh's PhD research and is great for church leaders and serious readers. *Grandparenting* is good for the casual reader and small group study.

The Power of a Godly Grandparent by Stephen and Janet Bly

Whether your grandchildren live across the country, down the street, or down the hall, *The Power of a Godly Grandparent* reveals how grandparents can be the most crucial family members grandchildren count on. You may or may not have material wealth to leave your grandchildren, but you can leave a rich heritage.

Grandparenting with a Purpose by Lillian Penner

God gives grandparents a sacred trust—an opportunity to imprint another generation with the message of His faithfulness. You can stand in the gap by being a godly example for your grandchildren and by praying for them. Regardless of how far away your grandchildren are, praying for them can bridge the distance between you and leave them with an inheritance more precious than gold.

Grandparenting with Grace by Larry McCall

This guidebook is designed to help grandparents apply the Gospel of Jesus Christ to the ministry of grandparenting. Every chapter in *Grandparenting with Grace* includes discussion questions and action steps to help you go deeper in your understanding of grandparenting and gain greater traction in your daily life as a grandparent. God has given us everything we need to grandparent, and He provides hope by applying the Gospel of Jesus Christ to situations that arise so you can impact your grandchildren for the glory of Christ.

As you can see, there are books to help you connect with your grandchildren and learn how to pass on a legacy of faith no matter their age or location. We hope these resources will be utilized to encourage and equip grandparents to pass on a heritage of faith!

Lynda Freeman is the very happy grandma to three grandsons who fill her heart with joy! She has written for VeggieTales, SuperBook, *Children's Ministry Magazine*, *Your Church Magazine*, and *HomeFront Magazine*, and is one of the contributing writers for *The Humongous Book of Bible Skits for Children's Ministry* from Group Publishing and *Pulse* from KidzMatters. Lynda is the creator/author for *Science, the Bible & Fun!*, *Generations Quest*, *Deeper In 4 Grandparents & Parents, Too!*, and *It Is Impossible to Spoil Grandchildren*, and is one of the founding members of the Legacy Coalition. In the fall of 2017 Lynda and seven wonderful grandmas started a new ministry, Grandmas with Heart, with the goal of providing resources that equip and empower grandmas (and grandpas and parents) to hand down a heritage of faith to the children they love. You will find Grandmas with Heart on Facebook.

10

Discipling Grandchildren: Fifteen Resources for Grandparents

BY JOSH MULVIHILL

Arny and Karen, grandparents of eighteen grandchildren, understand that there is a big difference between living one's later years for indulgent pursuits versus intentional purposes. They would be the first to tell you they aren't perfect grandparents, but they believe their example is one grandparents would benefit from hearing about.

Like most grandparents, Arny and Karen enjoy spending time with their children and grandchildren. Together, they like to camp, ski, hike, knit, even build skateboard racks. Sunday nights they drop off two grandsons at youth group; they make it a priority to see each family unit four to six times a year, and every other summer the entire family sets up tents and trailers on their property for an extended gathering.

Arny and Karen work hard to establish healthy relationships and create fun memories, but these are not the only reason they spend time with grandchildren. "We have a grandparenting motto: That the Lord would find us faithful. We want to pass on to our children what was passed to us," they say. Arny will passionately tell you, "We don't want to be the couple walking the shore picking up seashells. We have a reason for living. This means our task as grandparents is not finished. Otherwise we would be home with the Lord."

Arny and Karen camp with a purpose. They hike with intentionality. They invest their time with an eye on the eternal. When they spend time with grandchildren, the activity becomes the means to a greater end. Arny and Karen use family activities to intentionally pass faith on to their grandchildren: "We have been studying the Old Testament with our grandchildren and believe it is really important to talk about the Lord with them as much as we can. We speak about the Lord often and make it clear God is part of our life, not just part of our Sunday. We love to tell stories. We love to recount things that have happened to us where we clearly see God's hand. Ebenezer moments. Many times our grandkids have heard these stories before. The younger ones may not have heard or understood them. The older ones have. And you would expect the older ones will say, 'I've heard this' and run away, but we've had times when they've said, 'No, we want to hear that story again.' I think part of being a grandparent is to be storytellers. Especially stories about how God has been faithful in our lives."

Teach and Tell

Arny and Karen are models worthy of imitation because they understand God gives grandparents the responsibility to teach their children and their children's children the commands of God and to "tell to the coming generation the glorious deeds of the Lord" (Deuteronomy 4:9; Psalm 78:4). In God's sovereign plan, He placed grandparents in the lives of grandchildren as another voice to proclaim the good news of the Gospel and to disciple them to maturity in Christ.

I hope Arny and Karen's example encourages you to assume a role that is more than emotional support, an extra-special baby-sitting service, or the dispenser of large amounts of sugar. I hope their example encourages you to intentionally invest in your grandchildren, "so that they should set their hope in God and not forget the works of God, but keep his commandments" (Psalm 78:7).

More Than the Last Line of Defense

Many grandparents believe the spiritual training of grandchildren is someone else's responsibility and operate as a strong spiritual presence only if no other person fulfills this role in the life of the grandchildren. In this way, grandparents see themselves as the last line of defense, not an active partner in the day-to-day disciple-making process. The result for many grandparents is a hands-off spiritual role that abdicates to other influencers and leaves them to assume the role as the "fun" grandparent.

God's role for grandparents is not contingent on adult children raising grandchildren in the Lord or conditional based on a grandchild's involvement at church. Whether your grandchildren have godly parents or ungodly parents and whether they go to church or don't, God's role for you does not change. God calls all grandparents to pass on a heritage of faith in Christ from one generation to the next. God wants you to intentionally use the time you have with grandchildren to help them know, love, and serve Christ.

Fifteen Resources

Once grandparents embrace their role as disciple-makers, the next question is almost always, "What resources are available to help me teach and tell my grandchildren about God?"

With hundreds of wonderful resources available, and many more written every year, how does a grandparent know which ones to utilize? After twenty years as a pastor to young people, and five children of my own, here are fifteen of my go-to resources for grandparents. For additional family discipleship resources visit GospelShaped Family.com.

Long Story Short and *Old Story New* by Marty Machowski

When I was a pastor I bought these books by the boxful for families at Grace Church. *Long Story Short (O.T.)* and *Old Story New (N.T.)* are two of the best family devotional books available today. Marty highlights the Gospel in every devotional, helps families read and discuss Scripture in ten minutes a day, and the books are suitable for preschool through the tween years.

The Bible's Big Story by James M. Hamilton Jr.
The Whole Story of the Bible in 16 Verses by Chris Bruno

These resources will help you teach your grandchildren the big picture of the Bible centered on Jesus Christ. *The Bible's Big Story* is perfect for children while *The Whole Story of the Bible in 16 Verses* is excellent for teenagers. Many young people are confused by the Bible and see it as nothing more than a big book of rules or an outdated religious journal of other people's God-experiences. These books will help your grandchildren see the unity of Scripture and follow its main themes from beginning to end.

My 1st Book of Questions and Answers by Carine MacKenzie

I give this book to first-time parents and grandparents to help them explain the main teachings of the Bible to preschool and early elementary-aged children in a simple yet profound way. Carine asks 114 questions, each with a short answer and Bible reference.

The Gospel for Children by John Leuzarder (grade school)

Bitesize Theology by Peter Jeffery (middle school)

Essential Truths of the Christian Faith by R. C. Sproul (high school)

It is my conviction that every grandparent and parent needs to be teaching children the core doctrines of the Christian faith. There are foundational truths in the Bible that every believer, young and old, needs to learn. Each of these books will help you teach the basics of faith in an age appropriate and easily accessible way to young people.

Leading Your Child to Christ: Biblical Direction for Sharing the Gospel by Marty Machowski (grade school)

What Is the Gospel? by Greg Gilbert (middle and high school)

One of the shocking findings of my PhD research is few grandparents are sharing the Gospel with their grandchildren. Proclaiming the Gospel is a critical aspect of every grandparent's role. If you want to know how to share the Gospel, these are helpful resources.

Roots Kids Worship by Josh Mulvihill, Dara Mann, and Peter Bourne

Roots Kids Worship teaches children the core truths of the Bible through music. It is sung by kids for kids with an energy and style that appeals to all ages and is part of an integrated curriculum that combines music, message, and memorization. Roots Kids Worship and curriculum is available at Gospel-ShapedFamily.com.

ESV Seek and Find Bible (grade school)

The Gospel Story Bible by Marty Machowski (preschool)

I am asked regularly to recommend a Bible for children and youth. My preference is a Bible that contains the actual text of Scripture. The *ESV Seek and Find Bible* is great for children once they can read. It is full text but contains lots of pictures and explanations children love. When a young person hits the middle school years, my encouragement is to purchase a leather-bound Bible for them. If you want to be the extra-cool grandparent, have their name engraved on the cover.

The Trailblazer Series by various authors

There is great value in teaching young people about heroes from church history and telling them of the work of God in each of these individuals' lives. There are over forty action-packed books that introduce great Christian heroes to young people. Great for read-alouds!

Facebook Pages

Excellent resources are available for Christian grandparents on Facebook. Go to the ministry page for Gospel Shaped Family, the Legacy Coalition, Renewanation, and the Christian Grandparent Network and like each page. Regular encouragement as well as resources, blogs, and videos will show up in your news feed.

God's Names, God's Promise, and *God's Battle* by Sally Michael

Sally has written a series of books that teach children who God is and how they are to live the Christian life. I use these books to help children develop a high view of a great God as well as help children who are facing problems in life (anxiety, anger, etc.). One key question every child must answer is this: "Does God exist for me or do I exist for Him?" These books will help young people love God and trust Him.

Grandparenting Resource Kits by the Legacy Coalition

We created four kits that provide ten biblically based, Christ-centered resources in each kit to help grandparents intentionally influence the next generation with the Gospel. The resource kits will equip you to have spiritual conversations and teach biblical truths in an age-appropriate and engaging way. We have one kit to help you disciple preschoolers, one for grade-schoolers, and one for teens. The fourth kit contains resources that explain the role of a grandparent and help you launch a grandparent ministry. The resource kits are available at legacycoalition .com.

How to Study Your Bible for Kids by Kay Arthur

How to Study the Bible by John MacArthur (middle school and high school)

These resources will help your grandchildren develop the spiritual habit of reading the Bible, so they can grow as followers of Jesus Christ. Kay Arthur encourages grade school children to be detectives and teaches how to observe, interpret, and apply Scripture based on a study of Titus. John MacArthur provides a concise and readable overview of the doctrine of

Scripture followed by suggestions on how to develop a habit of reading the Bible daily.

The Wingfeather Saga by Andrew Peterson

I have included a number of content-heavy resources in this list, so this recommendation will appeal to those who like fiction. If you like the *Chronicles of Narnia*, you will love *The Wingfeather Saga*. It is in the same vein, with shadows that point to Christ, but set in another world with lots of adventure. My children couldn't get enough, and many nights we read for hours at a time, late into the evening. This is a great series to purchase and read aloud to your grandchildren when they come over and then cook cheesy chowder soup for dinner (one of the meals from the book)!

Preparing Children for Marriage by Josh Mulvihill

A critical topic children are confronted with at very young ages—one that is not covered in any of the other resources mentioned on this list. This book will help you teach preschoolers through high schoolers the truths of Scripture regarding God's definition of marriage, the role of a husband and wife, biblical manhood and womanhood, dating, purity, and more. A section in the book covers how to navigate this topic as a grandparent.

Biblical Worldview Toolkit by Renewanation

I created a resource that is Bible-based and Christ-centered to help families, churches, and schools intentionally teach the next generation key truths of Scripture. The toolkit includes approximately ten resources to help you shape the beliefs of your grandchildren so they develop a deep, lasting, and culture-transforming faith in Jesus. These resources will equip you to integrate biblical truth into your home and impress God's Word into young hearts. The toolkit is available at Renewanation.org.

Josh Mulvihill is the executive director of Church and Family Ministry at Renewanation, where he equips parents and grandparents to disciple their family and consults with church leaders to help them design Bible-based, Christ-centered children's, youth, and family ministries. Josh has served as a pastor for nearly twenty years, is a founding member of the Legacy Coalition, and has a PhD from the Southern Baptist Theological Seminary. He is the author of *Biblical Grandparenting*, *Preparing Children for Marriage*, and *Rooted Kids Curriculum and Worship*. Josh and his wife, Jen, live in Victoria, Minnesota, and have five children. For family discipleship resources, visit GospelShapedFamily.com.

More Foundational Grandparenting Resources

With depth and relevance, Dr. Josh Mulvihill helps you speak wisdom and godliness into the lives of your grandchildren. Here he gives you all you need to invest spiritually in your grandkids, from sharing with unbelieving grandkids to discipling them to a mature faith. Perfect for individual use, small groups, or Sunday school classes.

Grandparenting by Dr. Josh Mulvihill

Ideal for pastors and church leaders as well as for use in seminary classrooms, this insightful leadership book places grandparenting ministry on a firm scriptural foundation. This resource will help you share how grandparents can navigate their role in the family amid the culture's misleading messages and reach the next generation with the Gospel.

Biblical Grandparenting by Dr. Josh Mulvihill

Featuring eight family ministry experts and over six hours of video content, you will find all you need to invest spiritually in your grandkids in this DVD resource. Perfect for individual use, small groups, or Sunday school classes.

Grandparenting DVD